ZORRO X 2

Bernardo Solano

BROADWAY PLAY PUBLISHING INC
224 E 62nd St, NY, NY 10065
www.broadwayplaypub.com
info@broadwayplaypub.com

First printing: September 2010
I S B N: 978-0-88145-439-0

Book design: Marie Donovan
Typographic controls: Adobe InDesign
Typeface: Palatino
Printed and bound in the U S A

ZORRO x 2 (originally titled ZORRO) was commissioned by, and had its first production at, Theatreworks (Artistic Director, Murray Ross; Producing Director, Drew Martorella) in Colorado Springs, CO, opening on 26 September 2007. The cast and creative contributors were:

EDDIE ....Geno Silva
DIEGO .... Justin Huen
FISK .... Robert Rais
HAYES... Ashley Crockett
OLIVIA .... Jessica Gisin-Mosley
JENNY..Jess Heinrichs
BOB..Nick Henderson
Ensemble ....Jessica Parnello, Will Atkinson, Fernando
              Troche, Tom Condas, Joe Kinnet, Katy Steurer

Director .... Robert Castro
Production stage manager ....Kari Martin
Set designer .... Michael Stansbery
Lighting designer ....Les Dickert
Costume designer.. Betty Ross
Sound designer.. Will Boschellia
Fight choreographer .... Geoff Kent

CHARACTERS & SETTING

EDDIE REYES/ZORRO
DIEGO CERVANTES/ZORRO
JOHN FISK/EL MONSTRUO
FRANCINE HAYS
OLIVIA BAKER
JENNY WINTERS
BOB

ENSEMBLE: MOVIE WATCHERS / STUDENTS / WORKERS /
EL INOCENTE / MEN IN WHITE COATS

Place: the Southwestern Desert & Academy of the Desert

Time: the present

SPECIAL THANKS

Murray Ross

Drew Martorella

Robert Castro

Geno Silva

Justin Huen

Zorro, Inc

Theatreworks

DEDICATION

for: Paula, Raphael & Lena

ACT ONE

Scene One

(Somewhere in the desert. An outdoor movie screening. MOVIE WATCHERS *have gathered with blankets, etc. The "movie" is about to begin.)*

MOVIE WATCHER 1: Dude, the movie's starting.

MOVIE WATCHER 2: Dude, I know.

MOVIE WATCHER 3: Shh.

(On the "screen" appear iconic Southwestern images: desert vistas, cacti, boulders...and a homeless person asleep under a blanket. A light and sound shift turns it into a nightmarish landscape just as EL INOCENTE *enters)*

EL INOCENTE: *Dios mio.* (*To homeless person*) *Hola, senor, disculpe. No soy de aqui. Me fui por una caminada, y pues... ahora estoy perdido.*

MOVIE WATCHER 1: Dude, you didn't tell me it was a foreign flick!

MOVIE WATCHER 2: I didn't?

MOVIE WATCHER 1: So what's he saying?

MOVIE WATCHER 2: He's lost.

MOVIE WATCHER 1: Duh, I know that.

MOVIE WATCHER 3 & 4: Shhh!

(Who we thought was the homeless person is actually El Monstruo *who throws off his blanket and brandishes a very sharp weapon)*

Movie Watcher 1: Yeah!

El Monstruo: *Buenas noches.*

El Inocente: *Que demonios! Por favor no me mate!!*

El Monstruo: *Lo sentiras por solamente un momento.*

(Movie Watcher 1 *elbows* Movie Watcher 2.)

Movie Watcher 1: What he say?!

Movie Watcher 2: (*Translating*) "It'll only hurt for a second."

(Suddenly, Zorro *appears in spectacular fashion and in complete regalia: black clothes, cape, hat, bandana wrapped around his head with only his eyes showing, and of course, a sword.)*

Movie Watcher 1: Yeah—Zorro!

Zorro: Monstruo. *Que sorpresa.*

El Monstruo: *Zorro. Veniste a danar mi noche?*

Zorro: *No le puedo permitir que destripe a gente inocente.*

El Monstruo: *Podrias. De veras, podrias.*

Movie Watcher 1: What, what, what??!!

Movie Watcher 2: Zorro said he can't let innocent people get gutted. The monster dude said "you could, you really could."

Movie Watcher 3: Shut up!

Movie Watcher 1 & 2: You shut up!

Zorro: *No, Monstruo, no en la presencia de los espiritus de este lugar.*

El Monstruo: *Los espiritus de este lugar se murieron hace mucho tiempo.*

(ZORRO *unsheathes his sword.*)

EL MONSTRUO: *Ay, Zorro...insistes en resolver nuestros desacuerdos con violencia. Siempre con violencia.*

ZORRO: *Es la unica manera con usted, Monstruo.*

EL MONSTRUO: *Entonces, asi es.*

(MOVIE WATCHER 2 *is about to translate.*)

MOVIE WATCHER 1: I know, I know—the monster dude said "you always gotta get all violent" and Zorro goes "it's the only way, monster dude."

(EL MONSTRUO *and* ZORRO *engage in a vicious swordfight.* ZORRO *lunges with his sword, the sword goes clean through* EL MONSTRUO...*and right into the body of* EL INOCENTE. *The blade has had no effect on* EL MONSTRUO, *but* EL INOCENTE *crumples to the ground...dead*)

ZORRO: *¿Que? ¿Ha muerto?*

EL MONSTRUO: *Muy bien.* (*To* EL INOCENTE) *¿Ves? ¿No te dije que lo sentiras por solamente un momento?*

(ZORRO *is devastated and drops his sword.* EL MONSTRUO *picks it up*)

EL MONSTRUO: (*Re: sword*) *¿No la necesitaras mas, no es cierto?*

ZORRO: *No.*

EL MONSTRUO: *Ay, Zorro. Pobre Zorro.*

(EL MONSTRUO *drags* EL INOCENTE *off.*)

ZORRO: (*Mumbling to himself*) *¿Porque? ¿Porque?* Why? Why...why...why...why?!!

(ZORRO *bursts through the "movie screen" and onto the stage. The* MOVIE WATCHERS *flee as the man playing* ZORRO *is now just a berserk homeless man. He hides under his blankets next to a shopping cart. A new dawn arises.* EDDIE REYES *awakes with a start. Was it all only a dream?*)

EDDIE: No!! (*Beat*) Aw, crap. (*He gathers his wits, notices his shopping cart's broken wheel*) Tornado. My trusted steed. Look at this leg of yours. I know...the pain is unbearable. We both know what I have to do. I'm going to take you to a slow moving river that will transport you to the land of equine spirits...you'll be well taken care of. And our time together...will be but a distant memory that I trust will bring a smile to your lips. (*As he wheels the limp shopping cart off...*) Wait. What am I doing? I can't abandon you in your time of need. Come, Tornado. I will tend to your injuries.

(EDDIE *exits with Tornado*)

Scene Two

(*Academy of the Desert. Construction sounds.* DIEGO CERVANTES *is about to enter Headmaster* HAYS*'s large office. His cell phone rings, he answers.*)

DIEGO: Hello?

VOICE: (*On phone*) Mister Cervantes, this is your landlord.

DIEGO: Thank you for calling, leave a message and I'll get back to you as soon as possible. Beeeeeep.

VOICE: Mister Cervantes, I know that's not your voice mail. Listen, you are four months behind in your rent, we can't go on like this.

DIEGO: But, Mister Lupus—

VOICE: No, no more excuses. You're a nice young man. You have very clean fingernails—but you have to pay to play in this life and it's time to pay cash money.

DIEGO: Mister Lupus, let me finish! I got a job!

VOICE: A job? Doing what, playing with computers like you do every night?

DIEGO: No, sir. I got a teaching job. At the Academy of the Desert.

VOICE: That stuck-up private school?

DIEGO: It's not so bad, Mister Lupus and yes, that's the place. I'm going to be teaching Computer Sciences.

VOICE: They going to pay you money?

DIEGO: Yes, sir. Not a lot, but enough to start paying you back.

VOICE: Oh. Okay. Just remember, I know people who know people who work with special "collection agencies..." You know what I'm saying? Hmmm?

DIEGO: Yes, sir.

VOICE: Good. Have a nice day, Diego.

(DIEGO *hangs up and moans. Lights up on* HAYS's *spacious office.* JOHN FISK, *the school's head of security, is there with an antique samurai sword practicing intricate moves.* DIEGO *knocks on the door.*)

FISK: Enter.

(DIEGO *enters.*)

FISK: Don't just stand there. Close the door.

DIEGO: Sorry, I'm here to see—

FISK: Headmaster Hays isn't here. I'm John Fisk, I run security for the school. (*He continues his thrusts and parries with an invisible opponent.*) You must be Cervantes, Diego.

DIEGO: Actually it's Diego Cervantes.

FISK: Actually I know that. (*He stops for a moment to show off his sword.*) Ever seen one of these before?

DIEGO: A sword?

FISK: This is no ordinary sword. This is an authentic daito-katana samurai sword. Samurai warriors believed it was the soul of their warriorship. After forging the blade, the sword tester would take it and cut through the bodies of corpses. The results of which were recorded on the nakago...that's this metal piece attaching the sword blade to the handle. Look... (*He shows it to* DIEGO.) Looks like they tested this one...a lot.

DIEGO: Wow. I didn't know that.

FISK: That's why I showed you. The samurai even gave their swords names. Want to know mine?

DIEGO: Big Johnnie?

FISK: Big Johnnie, that's good. That's not it. (*Beat*) It's Peacemaker.

DIEGO: P-p-p-peacemaker. I like that.

FISK: I've never had to actually use it. I pray to God I never have to. I am in my core a man of peace. Hence...

DIEGO: Peacemaker.

FISK: Smart boy. So, you're the computer whiz. I know all about you.

DIEGO: (*Concerned*) You do?

FISK: You went to school here. They called you the "Geek of Geeks". Must've been hard being so socially incompetent. So identified with your reputation they created a special yearbook category for you: most likely to marry a computer.

DIEGO: Yes, sir. That was...difficult.

FISK: And after you graduated...poof...you disappeared. What happened?

DIEGO: It's hard to explain.

FISK: It always is, isn't it? (*Beat*) So why are you really here, Mister Cervantes? If you could afford to go to this school, you surely don't need the chicken scratch we're offering you. That is, unless...you spent your trust fund? On what? Computers? Pictures of women on computers? Men? Hmm?

DIEGO: I don't feel so good.

FISK: What's wrong, bad taco?

(HAYS *enters.* FISK's *demeanor changes.*)

FISK: Headmaster.

HAYS: Fisk. What are you doing in my office?

FISK: Welcoming our new teacher, ma'am.

HAYS: I see. (*To* DIEGO) Welcome, welcome, welcome! I truly appreciate your joining our little family. I must say, when I saw that you were a Cervantes and an alumnus, I knew that the interview wouldn't be necessary. "Hire him!" I said. Isn't that what I said, Fisk?

FISK: Yes, ma'am, that's almost exactly what you said.

HAYS: Since I took over last year there have been a few changes around here—have you noticed?

DIEGO: It looks like some construction's about to begin.

HAYS: Some? *Lots* of construction, my young friend. The Board and I have secured quite a large sum of money to spruce this place up. Fix the grounds. Erect a few new buildings. A complete make-over, if you will. And thus usher Academy of the Desert into the twenty-first century. What do you think of that?

DIEGO: It's...great.

HAYS: Yes, they say you were always a master of understatement.

FISK: Like his personality.

HAYS: (*Annoyed with* FISK) Yes, well...that was years ago. Now...now you've matured into a fine young man. At the prime of your riches—I mean, the richness that maturity brings to one's life. I imagine that your decision to teach here is primarily about wanting to give back to the school that nurtured you to adulthood. I certainly can't imagine it's because you need the work!

(HAYS *laughs heartily.* DIEGO *half-heartedly joins her. As she speaks, his demeanor gradually changes: his shoulders droop, his eyes squint, a nervous tick or two develops—it's as if he's regressing back to his old "geek" personality.*)

HAYS: Look out the window, Diego. Look at all those workers out there. They have mouths to feed. Rent to pay. Remittances to send back to sunny Mexico. And who is going to provide the money for them to do these things? The Academy of the Desert. Thanks to certain corporations. Certain loans. Certain generous private donors...perhaps your own family one day. (*Beat*) We've reached out to your father, you know. But our letters remain unanswered. Perhaps you'll consider acting as our intermediary? Then again, maybe you'll consider cutting a check of your own one of these days?

(*The transformation is complete.* DIEGO *is now uber-geek.*)

FISK: (*Indicating* DIEGO) Ma'am...

HAYS: Are you all right, Diego?

DIEGO: Y-y-yes.

HAYS: (*A little unnerved*) Yes, well...you must be tired. You certainly look tired. Why don't we table this for now?

DIEGO: Okay.

HAYS: I'll see you tomorrow—first day of classes, I hope you're ready!

DIEGO: Mm-mm. (*He exits like a mollusk.*)

FISK: Did you see that?

HAYS: You know what they say...hard as they try, some people never change.

FISK: Yeah, that might be so, but...I don't trust him.

HAYS: John, you and that "special ops" brain of yours. You wouldn't trust your own mother.

FISK: And for good reason, the bitch tried to trade me for drugs when I was ten.

HAYS: Be that as it may, last time I checked I was in charge here. So that means you...

FISK: Follow orders.

HAYS: Correct. (*Beat*) Kiss me.

FISK: Yes, ma'am.

(HAYS *and* FISK *kiss. She enjoys herself far more than he.*)

Scene Three

(*School grounds. First day of school.* DIEGO *enters carrying multiple items: backpack, computer bag, bag lunch, etc. Classic bungling and juggling routine.* JENNY WINTERS, *a student, enters—she's a younger version of him. The bungling and juggling is multiplied by two. Many "sorry"s and "I think that's mine" and "Oh! Let me help!" from both, ending in a crescendo of items falling to the ground.*)

JENNY: I'm so sorry, I'm really sorry, I really am!

DIEGO: It's okay, really it's okay, it really is!

JENNY: Really?

DIEGO: Really.

JENNY: I'm Jenny Winters. I'm a student.

DIEGO: I'm Diego Cervantes. I'm the new—

JENNY: Computer Sciences teacher. Oh, my gosh, you're a legend. It's an honor, sir.

DIEGO: Hey, I'm no "sir". Call me Diego.

JENNY: We're not allowed to do that, sir.

DIEGO: Really? Who started that rule?

JENNY: Headmaster Hays', sir.

(*Several day laborers/*WORKERS *enter, followed by* FISK.)

JENNY: (*Seeing* FISK) I gotta go.

DIEGO: What's the big hurry?

JENNY: Fisk. Last year, he just looked at me and I peed in my pants. Bye, sir.

(JENNY *exits.* DIEGO *recedes into the background and watches the following.*)

FISK: Okay, this is it. See that tree over there?

WORKER: Yes.

FISK: I want you to dig it up and move it over there.

(*Another worker,* BOB, *speaks up.*)

BOB: Why?

FISK: Why? What's your name?

BOB: Bob.

FISK: Bob, what kind of name is that? You don't look like a Bob.

BOB: Its name they call me. You call me Bobby.

FISK: No, thanks, "Bob". Look, do any of you guys remember me asking to see your green card?

BOB & WORKERS: No, sir.

FISK: Do you want me to?

BOB & WORKERS: No, sir.

(EDDIE *enters, taking his time, as if out for a stroll.*)

FISK: So you're going to move that tree from over there to over here. Right, Bob?

BOB: Right, boss.

(FISK *notices* EDDIE.)

FISK: (*To* EDDIE) Hey, you, straggler, if you don't want to work you can just walk on back to the Home Depot where I found you.

EDDIE: I think you have mistaken me for someone else. A relative of yours, perhaps?

FISK: I don't have any relatives who hang out at Home Depots.

EDDIE: Then maybe we have met before? Did we go to school together?

FISK: Doubtful. But your English is pretty good. Why are you with this crowd?

EDDIE: So as not to be lonely. Don't you have a crowd?

FISK: No.

EDDIE: Then you must be very lonely.

FISK: I don't like the way you're twisting my words, buddy.

EDDIE: Oh, so I'm your buddy! That means we're friends. So we did go to school together! *Amigos*, meet my old friend—what's your name again?

FISK: (*Re:* EDDIE) Moron.

EDDIE: My old friend Moron!

FISK: Ok, that's enough!

(FISK *grabs* EDDIE *roughly by the lapel.*)

EDDIE: Can you hit this side of my nose—that'll make it straight again.

(FISK *is about to oblige when* DIEGO *steps in.*)

DIEGO: Excuse me.

FISK: What?!

DIEGO: Excuse me, Mister Fisk?

FISK: Can't you see I'm about to turn this guy's face into ground round?

DIEGO: Yes, sir, but—

EDDIE: You didn't mention food—I'd be happy to stay for lunch.

FISK: (*To* DIEGO) Get out of my way.

DIEGO: I would really like to, but—

(FISK *moves to punch* EDDIE, *but trips over* DIEGO's *foot and crashes into* EDDIE, *knocking all three to the ground.*)

DIEGO: Sorry!

(FISK *leaps to his feet.*)

FISK: You idiot!

DIEGO: (*To* EDDIE) Are you all right?

(DIEGO *helps* EDDIE *to his feet.*)

EDDIE: I am now. (*To* FISK) I am deeply sorry, Mister Fisk. I am new to this neck of the woods and have not yet learned the quaint customs of your simple ways.

FISK: Don't even talk to me. (*To* DIEGO) You, too. (*To* WORKERS) Come on, I'll show you where the tools are.

(BOB *and the* WORKERS *follow* FISK *offstage.*)

DIEGO: My name is Diego.

EDDIE: *Mucho gusto.* Today my name is Eddie.

DIEGO: What about tomorrow?

EDDIE: Tomorrow is another day. *Ven.* Let me see your eyes.

DIEGO: Why?

EDDIE: It is imperative I see them now. Come close.

(EDDIE *looks deep into* DIEGO's *eyes.*)

EDDIE: Just as I suspected.

DIEGO: What is it? What do you see?

EDDIE: I can't say. Not yet. What I can say is that I need to be here. Close to you. Can you get me a job?

DIEGO: After what just happened, I doubt it.

EDDIE: You must do this.

DIEGO: Why is it so important you work here?

EDDIE: The future of humankind depends on it. Okay, maybe not the future of humankind in a global sense, but certainly a local one. And you are the key to it all.

DIEGO: Me?

EDDIE: You. You are the one.

DIEGO: (*Intrigued and a little intimidated*) I'm the one? That is, if I get you a job.

EDDIE: Precisely.

DIEGO: And then suddenly I'm some kind of hero, huh?

EDDIE: *Pues*, not so suddenly, but, yes. You would be. (*Beat*) Don't you want justice?

DIEGO: Well, yeah...

EDDIE: Don't you want to give strength to the weak?

DIEGO: I guess....

EDDIE: To heal the wounds that putrify the soul of humanity?

DIEGO: I don't know if I'd put it that way...

EDDIE: To make right what has gone wrong?

DIEGO: Is that possible?

EDDIE: It's not impossible. And once and for all...to be able to look into the mirror and like what you see?

(*Something in* DIEGO *has changed.* FISK *enters.*)

DIEGO: Mister Fisk! Can I speak to you?

FISK: Only if you really have to.

DIEGO: I do.

(DIEGO *takes* FISK *aside.*)

DIEGO: (*Indicating* EDDIE) That man...

FISK: You mean that moron?

DIEGO: Yes, him. He needs a job.

FISK: After what just happened, you think I'm going to give him a job?

DIEGO: Uh...yeah.

FISK: And why would I do that?

DIEGO: Because if you don't...I'll quit...and I'll take my money with me. I don't think Headmaster Hays would be very happy about that.

FISK: Do I detect a spine in that body of yours?

DIEGO: No, I just, um...he deserves a break, that's all.

(*Pause*)

FISK: All right. He can work here. Be a janitor—I'm sure the smell won't bother him.

DIEGO: Thank you.

FISK: Yeah, just don't forget I did you this favor.

(EDDIE *blows* FISK *kisses, which makes him leave faster.*)

DIEGO: (*To himself*) I did it. I actually did it.

(EDDIE *comes up to* DIEGO.)

EDDIE: You sound surprised.

DIEGO: You're a janitor.

EDDIE: Janitor? ...Yes. It's perfect. No one will ever suspect.

DIEGO: Suspect what?

EDDIE: My true identity, what else?

DIEGO: Okay, I'm hooked. What is this true identity of yours?

(Pause. EDDIE *makes sure no one is listening.)*

EDDIE: *Mira.* Can I trust you with my life?

DIEGO: Um...I don't know...I guess.

EDDIE: I believe you. *(Beat)* I am Zorro.

DIEGO: No, you're not.

EDDIE: I am. I am Zorro.

DIEGO: Zorro is a character in a movie.

EDDIE: Not just one movie, my friend. Many. And more than one television series. Several books, too. But do you know who those book and movie Zorro's were based on?

DIEGO: Let me guess. You?

EDDIE: In the flesh!

DIEGO: Okay, so much for the future of humankind.

EDDIE: Your doubts are well-founded. There are countless cases of ordinary people purporting to be notable figures from the annals of history. Napoleon. Gandhi. Elvis.

DIEGO: And now Zorro.

EDDIE: Except I am no pretender to the throne. I am the genuine article.

DIEGO: Of a fictional character.

EDDIE: It's a mystery, isn't it?

DIEGO: Right. Look, I have to get to class.

EDDIE: Yes, of course. The student is also a teacher. It's perfect.

DIEGO: What do you mean "the student is also a teacher?"

EDDIE: In due time, my young charge. In due time.

DIEGO: (*humoring him*) So. Good luck with your new job, Mister...Zorro.

EDDIE: And you with yours!

(EDDIE *runs, leaps, and bounds off stage.*)

DIEGO: How'd he do that?

Scene Four

(*Classroom.* DIEGO *lectures to the class and/or the audience.* JENNY *is the only one paying attention to* DIEGO.)

DIEGO: The presentation of phrase elements depends on the user agent. Speech synthesizer user agents may change the synthesis parameters, such as volume, pitch and rate accordingly. (*He suspects no one is listening.*) How many of you have ever gone hungry? How many of you have pretended not to see a homeless person right in front of you? How many of you pick your nose when nobody's watching? (*He gives up.*)

JENNY: Why did you stop, sir? It's so amazing what you were saying. It just boggles my mind.

DIEGO: Well, I think you're the only one. (*Beat*) I thought you said I was a legend.

JENNY: Well, yeah, but...now you're a teacher. That cancels everything out. But I like to think that there's more to people than the labels we give them.

DIEGO: (*Beat*) So, what are they all doing?

JENNY: I M-ing. YouTube. My Space. Facebook. I-Tunes. Porn.

DIEGO: All that?

JENNY: And then some.

DIEGO: What's your story, Jenny?

JENNY: I don't have a story, sir.

DIEGO: Sure, you do. Everybody has a story.

JENNY: You wouldn't want to hear it, it's pretty boring.

DIEGO: Been there, done that. Doing that. Clearly.

JENNY: It's okay, Mister Cervantes. I understand.

DIEGO: I think you do.

(The bell rings. The class empties in about a second. JENNY *lingers behind.)*

JENNY: Can I ask you a question, sir?

DIEGO: Sure.

JENNY: Is it true that you're rich—I mean, like super rich?

(Pause)

DIEGO: What if I told you I was dirt poor? Would it make a difference?

JENNY: Not to me, sir.

DIEGO: *(Admiringly)* Jenny, you must be from another planet.

JENNY: Same planet as you, sir.

*(*EDDIE *enters with a bucket and mop; he uses it like a rifle and bayonet.)*

EDDIE: *(To* JENNY*)* Who goes there?!

JENNY: Huh?

EDDIE: What's the password?

JENNY: Uh...

DIEGO: It's okay, Jenny, he's...

EDDIE: Quick or I'll run you through!

JENNY: Insane?

EDDIE: Close enough! You may pass.

(JENNY *high-tails it out of there.*)

DIEGO: Why'd you scare her like that?

EDDIE: Give her a harmless taste of it now, she won't be lured by the siren call of violence later.

DIEGO: Okay.

EDDIE: How's your first day been?

DIEGO: Terrible. How's yours?

EDDIE: Terribly edifying. (*Indicating* DIEGO's *classroom*) I had no idea education had come to this. The natives are resting and the machines are running the world.

DIEGO: I bet Zorro would have something to say about it.

EDDIE: I just did.

(OLIVIA BAKER *enters, a paper in her hand.*)

OLIVIA: Excuse me!

EDDIE: I'm a janitor. Eddie the Janitor. No relation to a certain caped crusader.

OLIVIA: Right.

(EDDIE *goes about his business.*)

EDDIE: Don't mind me, just going about my janitorial business. (*He recedes into the background, eavesdropping.*)

OLIVIA: (*To* DIEGO) You must be the new teacher... Mister Cervantes?

DIEGO: (*Barely audible*) Mm-mm.

OLIVIA: Will you sign this, please?

DIEGO: Wh...wh...wha...

OLIVIA: What is it?

(DIEGO *nods yes.*)

OLIVIA: It's a petition that you just have to sign. Oh, I'm sorry. My name is Olivia Baker, I'm a history teacher here. So are you going to sign or not?

DIEGO: ...There aren't any signatures.

OLIVIA: Yes, that's true.

DIEGO: I'm the first one?

OLIVIA: No, not exactly. (*Beat*) You're the last. But you'd be the first to sign.

DIEGO: (*Reading off the paper*) "We, the faculty of Academy of the Desert, strongly object to the oppressive, repressive, and regressive treatment of the day laborers currently working on the Academy Re-Construction Project."

OLIVIA: I know it's just your first day and all, but...do you have any idea how they're being treated?

DIEGO: I do. (*Beat*) Why didn't any of the faculty sign it?

OLIVIA: Because they're afraid Hays would fire them.

DIEGO: Would she?

OLIVIA: Yes. But not if everyone signed it. She can't run the school without teachers.

(DIEGO *wants to sign it.* EDDIE *gets his attention, gives him a signal to not sign it.*)

DIEGO: (*Meant for* EDDIE) Why not?

OLIVIA: Because you need teachers to teach, that's why not.

(EDDIE *makes the "Z" sign of Zorro with his mop somewhere that* DIEGO *can see.*)

DIEGO: I don't know....

EDDIE: (*Faking a cough and blurting out*) Yes, you do!

(OLIVIA *looks at* EDDIE)

EDDIE: Bad taco. Sorry.

OLIVIA: Well?

DIEGO: Sorry, I...I can't sign it.

OLIVIA: So the rumors are true: you were born without a spine. Have a nice day, Mister Cervantes.

(DIEGO *watches her leave.* EDDIE *nods approvingly.*)

DIEGO: Why'd I do that?

EDDIE: Because it's what Zorro would do.

DIEGO: I don't get it.

EDDIE: *Oye.* If you'd done your homework you'd know that if Zorro acted like Zorro in his daily life, everyone would know his identity. The forces of oppression and injustice would find him in an instant, incarcerate him, torture him, and in so doing, prevent him from undermining their nefarious plots to rule the world. And more importantly, prevent him from inspiring the oppressed. You see, as long as Zorro remains free, the people can imagine the day that they too will be free. Thus they are inspired to work toward realizing that elusive yet oh-so-real goal because one man...Zorro... is among them, leaving his mark for all to see. (*He slowly walks around* DIEGO.) *Mira.* A few minutes ago you could barely balance your body over your feet. Your heart mumbled. Your dreams stuck in the muck of mediocrity. But now. You stand taller. Your feet are firmly planted. Your heart sings. Your dreams float toward the firmament. (*Beat*) It is good you let me see this side of you.

DIEGO: You see all this...in me?

EDDIE: I do.

DIEGO: How?

EDDIE: Because I am Zorro. And Zorro can see things other men can't. Now, let us speak of your other self...

DIEGO: The one people ridicule?

EDDIE: Why do you say that?

DIEGO: I'm a geek. I know that. I've always known it.

EDDIE: Define geek.

DIEGO: Geek is a guy who knows a lot about something. Math, Science, nano-technology-whatever everyone else could care less about. When other kids were worrying about who's seen with who, who takes who to the prom...I was writing computer code. Whenever the bullies were bored, they'd come looking for me for a little entertainment. Ever heard of that movie, "Carrie?"

EDDIE: (*Rapid fire*) Stephen King novel, directed by Brian de Palma, starring Sissy Spacek. At the homecoming dance, bucket of pig's blood dumped on Carrie's head, Carrie kills the whole school.

DIEGO: Yeah, I guess you have heard of it. Anyway, I'm Carrie, except it wasn't pig's blood and I didn't kill the whole school. I just disappeared the day after graduation. (*Beat*) I was "less than" and that's all they needed to know.

EDDIE: You were different. Different scares people, and that makes them do stupid things. Anyway, you shouldn't resent that part of yourself. You must love it. And then use it. It is the cloak that shields you from prying eyes.

DIEGO: What about you? Don't you have...a "cloak"?

EDDIE: Of course I do. They think I'm addled. The town idiot. A buffoon. A man who talks to himself. A man who sees things that other men can't.

DIEGO: Okay, maybe you're not exactly who I thought you were.

(*A crashing sound from outside.* EDDIE *reacts by taking cover in an almost feral way.*)

EDDIE: Take cover!

DIEGO: I think it was just somebody dropping something outside.

EDDIE: No! It was him!

DIEGO: No, it was just—

EDDIE: El Monstruo!

DIEGO: The Monster?

EDDIE: Hide me, please, hide me!

DIEGO: There's nothing out there, Eddie.

EDDIE: You don't understand! He's found me! I've been hiding a long time, playing like I'm crazy, fooling everybody, thinking he'd never look for me in all those places!

DIEGO: Eddie, there's nobody out there except for some workers.

(EDDIE *is on his hands and knees—he seems to be losing whatever grip on reality he had.*)

EDDIE: *No lo oyes?!* He's out there!! And he found me because of you! Because I came out of hiding for you! This is what I get for trying to help!

DIEGO: I'm going for help—

EDDIE: No, don't leave me!

DIEGO: Okay, okay.

(EDDIE *grabs and holds on to* DIEGO *for dear life.*)

EDDIE: He's dead! He's dead because of me!

DIEGO: Who—El Monstruo?

EDDIE: No! The guy! The guy! El Inocente! I killed him!

DIEGO: It's okay, Eddie. You're here now. With me. You're here.

EDDIE: Don't let go. Don't let go. Don't let go. (*This time, directly to* DIEGO) Don't let go.

Scene Five

(*School grounds.* BOB *and the* WORKERS *are carrying long planks of wood—a commedia latzi of people narrowly avoiding catastrophe.* DIEGO *enters, stops to watch.*)

DIEGO: (*To* BOB) Can I help?

BOB: No, teacher. Very kind, but this not your work. Is okay.

DIEGO: You don't understand. I want to help.

BOB: There are ways, teacher. This not one.

DIEGO: Here, just let me—

(DIEGO *causes the catastrophe and* WORKERS *topple every which way.*)

DIEGO: I am so sorry.

BOB: Is okay.

(DIEGO *takes note of the condition of the plank.*)

DIEGO: This wood is rotten.

(*We see or simply hear* FISK *with a megaphone.*)

FISK: Mister Cervantes. Mister Cervantes! Step away from the foreign born worker. I said—

BOB: Okay, boss, he go now!

(DIEGO *reluctantly exits.* BOB *and* WORKERS *also exit.*)

Scene Six

(HAYS' *office. A few minutes later.* DIEGO *enters.*)

DIEGO: Headmaster Hays? I'd like to ask you about the Reconstruction Project... (*He notices* HAYS' *computer, he goes over to it.*) She shouldn't leave her computer on like this. Anybody could come and... (*He looks at the screen.*) Whoa. That is the ugliest screensaver I have ever seen. (*He suddenly notices some papers on the desk. One in particular gets his attention.*) Bank statement. The Cayman Islands? (*He finds another piece of paper*) What is this? (*Reading*) Payroll. That's what they're getting? That's highway robbery. (*Beat*) A highway headed straight to the Caymans.

(FISK *is just offstage, on his way to* HAYS's *office.*)

FISK: Francine, we need to talk!

(DIEGO *quickly puts the papers back, pretends to be looking at the screensaver just as* FISK *enters.*)

FISK: Oh. Cervantes. What are you doing here?

DIEGO: I came to see Headmaster Hays and, uh...the screensaver got my attention.

(FISK *goes up to the computer, looks at the screen.*)

FISK: Yeah, it's beautiful, huh?

DIEGO: It's terr...ibly beautiful.

FISK: Took it myself.

DIEGO: No kidding. (*Beat*) Looks like Headmaster Hays got tied up somewhere.

FISK: Yeah, she just might be. With a big smile on her lips.

(DIEGO *laughs nervously.* FISK *is at the window, looking out at the* WORKERS.)

FISK: You ever gut a pig?

DIEGO: No.

FISK: Actually it's pretty easy. You cut down the belly, from inside. With your other hand you hold the guts away from the point of your knife. Then you cut through the belly fat all the way down to the sternum. Next, cut the meat between the legs. By now the guts will be bulging out of the body. At some point there may be a flow of greenish liquid from the neck. This is just the cud, nothing to worry about.

DIEGO: I'm sure that's true.

FISK: (*Still looking at the* WORKERS) Chopping the skull with an axe works for getting out the brains. You remove the ears, eyes, nose—anything that doesn't look like meat or bone. I use the head meat for scrapple, tamale meat and pozole...used to use some in liverwurst, but now I just get it at Whole Foods. (*Beat*) Maybe one of these days you'd like to watch me?

DIEGO: Watch you?

FISK: Me and the pig. That is, unless you yourself are interested in becoming somebody's scrapple.

DIEGO: No. I'm not.

FISK: And you're not planning on coming back in here alone again, are you?

DIEGO: No, sir.

FISK: Good. I'll walk you out.

(FISK *and* DIEGO *exit.*)

Scene Seven

(DIEGO's *classroom.* EDDIE *is practicing martial arts moves.*
He's rusty, but still has skills. DIEGO *enters, ashen from his*
encounter with FISK. EDDIE *quickly stops.*)

EDDIE: Afternoon.

DIEGO: Where have you been?

EDDIE: Licking my wounds. (*Beat*) I want to apologize
for the other day.

DIEGO: It's okay.

EDDIE: You could've sent me away.

DIEGO: How could I send Zorro away? I'd have to
move on to Spiderman or Batman—and we all know
they don't speak Español.

EDDIE: You made a joke. That's wonderful! That was a
joke, right?

DIEGO: Yeah, it was. (*Beat*) But you can't tell anybody
else you're Zorro, okay? And that's not a joke.

EDDIE: *Bueno.* (*Beat*) You look like road-kill.

DIEGO: I feel like it.

EDDIE: Fisk?

DIEGO: How'd you know?

EDDIE: I can smell his stink, it's on your clothes, trying
to get inside your body. Infect your soul.

DIEGO: Wow. I think you're right.

EDDIE: What happened?

DIEGO: Well, you wouldn't believe what I just found in
Hays' office.

EDDIE: Try me.

DIEGO: You know the workers? She's paying them
sub-standard wages. Not only that, she's using cheap,

rotten materials. She's not just trying to save a buck, she's pocketing the extra money for herself. I can smell her stink from here.

EDDIE: All this seems to bother you.

DIEGO: Hell, yes, it bothers me! You can't treat people like that! Those men are working their butts off for chicken scratch! Plus they'll probably get the blame when those buildings eventually collapse!

EDDIE: It'll never get to that. Because she'll have them deported long before.

DIEGO: Oh, my God, you're right!

EDDIE: So what do you want to do?

DIEGO: Fight her! Stop it from happening!

EDDIE: The cause is just.

DIEGO: Exactly! People need to know that justice is still possible!

EDDIE: Yes. Yes. But how? You're just a young, inexperienced teacher who's afraid of losing his job.

(*Pause*)

DIEGO: What about Zorro?

EDDIE: *¿Y que?* What about him?

DIEGO: You say you're him. Bring him back.

EDDIE: Do you mean that?

DIEGO: Yes.

EDDIE: But you yourself saw me. What I've become. I can't be Zorro anymore.

DIEGO: Sure you can.

EDDIE: I would either go insane. Or die. (*Beat*) No.

(DIEGO *paces*.)

DIEGO: What about me?

EDDIE: You? You think you can be Zorro?

DIEGO: Yeah, why not? You did it.

EDDIE: I did it because I saw a need and I had no choice but to address that need.

DIEGO: Yeah, well, I see a need, too.

EDDIE: We all do. Doing something about it is another story.

DIEGO: I'm ready to do something. Train me. Show me the ways of Zorro.

EDDIE: People don't do heroic things to be heroes.

DIEGO: I know that.

EDDIE: Nor do they do it to escape their daily lives.

DIEGO: I know.

EDDIE: You might lose everything you have.

DIEGO: I know.

EDDIE: You might even lose your life.

DIEGO: I know.

EDDIE: And still you'd take on the mantle of Zorro?

DIEGO: Yes.

EDDIE: Even though I believe you have what it takes, I can't guarantee that you'll succeed.

DIEGO: I know that. I just...my life...it won't...I have to try. (*Beat*) Please be my teacher?

EDDIE: I've only been waiting for you to ask. (*Beat*) If we are to do this...you must take a solemn oath. Will you?

DIEGO: Yes.

(*The following is accompanied by a physical ritual that involves a mop or broomstick*)

EDDIE: A warrior must learn how to fight. But he does
so with the expressed hope that he will never have
to resort to it. It only begets pain and loss and great
suffering. Violence in the extreme is a line that must
never be crossed. Will you swear to this?

DIEGO: I swear.

EDDIE: So be it. (*He finishes the ritual.*)

DIEGO: That's it?

EDDIE: Not exactly.

(*A circle of light surrounds* EDDIE *and* DIEGO.)

DIEGO: Where'd that come from?

(EDDIE *uses the mop/broom to take* DIEGO's *feet out from
under him and he crashes to the ground*)

DIEGO: Hey!! Owww!!

EDDIE: Your first fight lesson has begun...Young Zorro.

DIEGO: You could've warned me.

EDDIE: Does the enemy say, "Oh, Hello, I'm about to
gut you"

DIEGO: He might.

EDDIE: Might is another word for dead.

(EDDIE *unscrews the mop and broom from their long sticks.
He throws one to* DIEGO.)

EDDIE: What do you have in your hands?

DIEGO: A broom handle.

EDDIE: Not anymore. These are quarterstaffs. (*As he
speaks he demonstrates the capabilities of the quarterstaff.*)
In old England, common folk couldn't afford expensive
weapons. Thus, the quarterstaff. Throughout the
Middle Ages, schools of "fence" taught foot soldiery,
self-defense and the use of weapons. In 1625, in Spain,
a gentleman from Devonshire pitted his quarterstaff

against three experts with rapiers. He defeated all three. Have I mentioned that I learned the art of the rapier at the Royal Court in Spain?

DIEGO: The Royal Court? In Spain?

EDDIE: *Pues si*, "in Spain"! Where else do you think I was when my father called me back to California?

DIEGO: California?

EDDIE: Yes, to the City of La Reina de los Angeles. A little backwater full of corrupt officials, ruthless soldiers and spineless caballeros.

DIEGO: Eddie, I have to tell you something. Since we've met, I've rented a couple of the Zorro movies, and, uh... what you're telling me...it's from the movies. The plot of a movie.

EDDIE: Yes. And they were good movies that were inspired by the exploits of the real Zorro. I don't begrudge them the right to commemorate my deeds to posterity. In fact I'm quite flattered. So, do you want to continue with the next phase of your lessons or do you want to argue about the reality of cinema?

DIEGO: (*Sighs*) Continue.

(*A light shift indicates a new lesson is beginning.*)

EDDIE: What are the five senses?

DIEGO: Sight, sound, taste, touch...and...uh...

(EDDIE *belches right in* DIEGO's *face*)

DIEGO: ...Smell.

EDDIE: Right. When a warrior is in battle, all five of his senses must be at their zenith. You should be able to smell your enemy's presence at a hundred feet, and know what he had for breakfast. See his muscles move and anticipate where his blow is intended. Hear his breathing, and know when fatigue is setting in to take advantage of it. The taste of your own sweat and blood to know the difference between them is the difference between life and death. The feel of your weapons, they are an extension of your body, your mind and your heart. They will do what you ask of them as long as you are pure in intention and noble in spirit. (*Beat*) Hello, I am about to gut you.

DIEGO: Wait!

EDDIE: No one waits! Defend yourself!

(EDDIE *attacks.* DIEGO *makes a feeble attempt to defend himself.* EDDIE *pins him and is poised to deliver the "death-blow".*)

DIEGO: I guess I flunked.

EDDIE: This isn't some *pinche* video game you learn in an hour. It takes time.

(*As* EDDIE *helps him up,* DIEGO *takes advantage and uses his quarterstaff to deck* EDDIE).

DIEGO: How's that?

EDDIE: Not bad. (*He decks* DIEGO *again.*) How's that?

Scene Eight

(DIEGO's *classroom. Two weeks later. He is alone, practicing with another improvised weapon.*)

DIEGO: (*To himself*) Be one with your weapon. Be one with your weapon. Be one with your weapon...

(DIEGO *attempts a difficult move as* OLIVIA *enters and sees him fail miserably, smacking himself hard.*)

OLIVIA: I hope you don't bruise easy.

DIEGO: Oh! (*Covering badly*) I, um...I was, uh...I have no idea what I was doing.

OLIVIA: That I believe. (*Beat*) What's changed? Something's different. Are you wearing platform shoes?

DIEGO: No.

OLIVIA: Hm. Well, anyway, even though you were a total wuss a couple weeks back, I at least sensed that you had the tiniest bit of sympathy for our cause.

DIEGO: (*Correcting her*) *Your* cause.

OLIVIA: (*Disgusted*) Why do I even bother? (*She starts to leave in a huff.*)

DIEGO: Wait!

OLIVIA: What?!

DIEGO: I agree with you that something should be done. That is, if it's true.

OLIVIA: It is true!

DIEGO: Do you have proof?

OLIVIA: Look. I represented the faculty on the Reconstruction Project Blue Ribbon Committee. We were adamant that we'd become an oversight committee once work began. There has been diddly squat for oversight. And every member of the committee has systematically been bullied and intimidated into not doing what was supposed to be our job. You're looking at the only person who hasn't given in.

DIEGO: I guess you don't get intimidated very easily.

OLIVIA: The only thing that intimidates me is me.

DIEGO: I wonder why they haven't fired you.

OLIVIA: I don't know. Well, actually...I sort of do know.

(FISK *enters with* BOB, *who is carrying some ridiculously heavy object—the more absurd, the better.*)

FISK: (*To* OLIVIA) There you are, I've been looking all over for you.

OLIVIA: Isn't that strange-I haven't been looking for you.

FISK: Bob?

BOB: Yes, boss?

FISK: Is that thing heavy?

BOB: Yes, boss.

FISK: Hmm. Why don't you take it outside, get yourself a cup of water.

BOB: Yes, boss. (*He exits with the incredibly heavy object*)

FISK: (*To* OLIVIA) Aren't you feisty today.

OLIVIA: Mister Fisk—

FISK: Now I'm Mister Fisk? That's not what you called me a few months ago.

OLIVIA: *That* was a moment of margarita madness that I'll regret for the rest of my life, the next one, and the one after that. And even then I'll ask myself if it wouldn't have been better to jump off a very high cliff.

FISK: What you mistake for wit is actually starting to rub me the wrong way.

DIEGO: I think I should go.

FISK: What's the matter, Cervantes? Never seen a lovers' quarrel?

OLIVIA: If you call it that again I will—

FISK: You'll what? (*Changing tactics*) You miss me, don't you? My awesome power scared you, I understand. You'll come back.

OLIVIA: For me to come back you'd have to feed me to the sharks, catch them, cook them and serve them for dinner.

FISK: Wonder what I should use for seasoning? Shake & Bake?

DIEGO: I think it's clear Ms Baker isn't interested in your company.

FISK: I think it's clear you need to stay out of this.

(FISK *pushes* DIEGO, *knocks him down easily.*)

FISK: Wow. Next time I'll just blow.

(DIEGO *considers fighting back, but changes his mind.*)

OLIVIA: Don't get up, Diego. He'll just hurt you worse. That's what he does.

(FISK's *phone rings, he looks at the number.*)

FISK: Gotta go. (*To* OLIVIA) See you in your dreams.

(FISK *exits.* OLIVIA *helps* DIEGO *to his feet.*)

OLIVIA: I'm so sorry.

DIEGO: It's okay.

OLIVIA: About Fisk...I'll never go back to T G I Fs for as long as I live.

DIEGO: I don't blame you.

OLIVIA: ...I gotta go. Papers to grade.

DIEGO: Yeah, I, uh...I have some work to do, too.

(OLIVIA, *confused by her feelings, exits.* DIEGO *is also flummoxed. A moment later* EDDIE *makes a terrific entrance.*)

EDDIE: Ready for your next lesson?

DIEGO: (*Re:* EDDIE's *entrance*) How'd you do that?

(*The circle of light re-appears.*)

DIEGO: And I still don't know how you do that.

EDDIE: It starts with this.

(EDDIE *grabs another object in room and pokes* DIEGO'*s belly.*)

DIEGO: Oww.

EDDIE: (*Poking at* DIEGO'*s head*) Or with this. (*Poking at* DIEGO'*s feet*) Or with these.

DIEGO: What are you doing?

EDDIE: Balance. Agility. Grace. The most skilled swordsmen have all of these. But not only in the heat of battle. They come in handy in all sorts of situations. Take Ms Baker, for example.

DIEGO: What about her?

EDDIE: You'd like to woo her, wouldn't you?

DIEGO: Woo?

EDDIE: (*Sensually*) Woo.

DIEGO: There's no way she'd go for me.

EDDIE: She'd go for Zorro.

(*Pause*)

DIEGO: When I was a student here...there was this girl—two grades up. She was so beautiful. Smart, too.

EDDIE: *Y?*

DIEGO: And I liked her—there, I said it, are you happy? So I told my father. He knew who she was. She was from a "bad" family from a "bad" part of town with a "bad" reputation. When I asked him what that meant, he wouldn't answer. He just went on about his business—making money. That's what he was good at. (*Beat*) And now he's the one who's—he lost it all. Everything. Mismanagement and—I'm pretty sure—outright fraud. He disappeared with everyone's money. And sooner or later everyone's going to know. (*Beat*) Why do people go from good to bad? Shouldn't it be the other way around?

(The circle of light disappears)

EDDIE: *Basta.* I quit.

DIEGO: What? What are you saying?

EDDIE: It's too much. What you want from me...it's too much.

DIEGO: Well, then, forget I told you.

EDDIE: I can't be your father, Diego.

DIEGO: I don't want you to be my father! I want you to be my teacher!

EDDIE: And that's what your father should have been!

DIEGO: Okay, I get it! I get what you're saying, but... these last few weeks...I have felt...so good...about myself...about... (*He grabs a sword or sword substitute and makes the Z with it.*) And how I look at things...at people—your fly's unzipped. (*Beat*) When my hand touches still water, it's like I see ever-expanding rings of cause and effect. That's all because of you.

EDDIE: No, it's you. It's always been there. You just needed a little help.

DIEGO: And I need a lot more of it. (*Beat*) What would you be doing if you weren't here teaching me? Picking through dumpsters? Talking to yourself? Letting yourself slowly die in some alley? Letting Zorro die with you.

EDDIE: Let Zorro die?

DIEGO: That's what you'd be doing. And that would be just as bad as what my father did.

EDDIE: *Que va!* It would be worse.

DIEGO: So. You still want to quit being my teacher?

EDDIE: No.

DIEGO: Okay. Shall we continue or would you rather argue about the merits of the i-Pad?

EDDIE: Continue.

(The circle of light appears again. EDDIE tosses DIEGO a blindfold.)

EDDIE: Put it on.

(DIEGO puts on the blindfold as EDDIE puts a box in front of DIEGO.)

EDDIE: There is a box before you. There are compartments within it. Each compartment holds an object. Touch the object, tell me what it is.

DIEGO: Okay. *(He reaches into the box, feels an object.)* Round. Fuzzy. Soft. A peach.

EDDIE: *Muy bien.* Continue.

(DIEGO reaches in again)

DIEGO: Hard. Has a handle. Owww! You put in a knife?!

EDDIE: Continue.

DIEGO: I can't believe you—

EDDIE: Continue!

DIEGO: Okay, okay. *(Reaching in)* Where is it? There's nothing in this compartment—wait, I feel something—owww, it bit me! What just bit me?!

EDDIE: That is for you to determine.

DIEGO: Oh. It's a rabbit. He's so warm. He's licking the finger he bit. Cool.

(The circle of light fades to black, and as it comes back up, DIEGO still has the blindfold on. But both he and EDDIE are holding rapier swords. EDDIE dictates fencing positions for DIEGO to practice.)

EDDIE: *En garde...*thrust...parry...*reposte...* (*Beat*) I'm hungry.

(EDDIE *sits and eats while he makes* DIEGO *do increasingly difficult combinations, until...*)

EDDIE: Take a break.

(EDDIE *and* DIEGO *sit in silence and eat together. It is a transcendent moment that illuminates the new depth of their friendship.*)

EDDIE: Listo?

DIEGO: Ready.

(EDDIE *stands.*)

EDDIE: Listen.

(EDDIE *slowly walks around the edge of the circle.* DIEGO *moves as well, always with his rapier ready.*)

EDDIE: *Bien. Bien.* Listen for my inhalation...the sound of the rapier moving through space.

(EDDIE *lunges at* DIEGO, *who quickly parries—deflecting* EDDIE'*s rapier.*)

EDDIE: *Eso.* Your turn to lunge.

(EDDIE *keeps moving.* DIEGO *tries to gauge where* EDDIE *is.*)

EDDIE: By the way, have I mentioned that you're an idiot? A coward. A spineless Mexican Hyphen American pendejo.

(DIEGO *loses his temper, lunges at* EDDIE *clumsily.*)

EDDIE: You let your temper cloud your judgment. You can't let that happen or you'll be defeated in a heartbeat.

DIEGO: I know.

EDDIE: Continue.

(EDDIE *moves,* DIEGO *gauges.*)

EDDIE: Oh, I forgot to add that you have no social graces, no redeeming characteristics of any kind, and... you're a geek. The geek of all geeks. Most likely to— (*His chest tightens.*) Ahhhh!

(EDDIE *goes to his knees.* DIEGO *rips off his blindfold, rushes over, holds* EDDIE *in his arms.*)

DIEGO: Eddie!

EDDIE: I'm fine. It's nothing.

DIEGO: Should I take you to the hospital?

EDDIE: No. No hospital. (*He places his hand on* DIEGO'*s chest.*) Your heart is strong enough for the two of us.

Scene Nine

(*The school grounds. Another day.* BOB *and the* WORKERS *are carrying large bags of concrete across the stage.* JENNY *is there eating her lunch.* BOB, *exhausted, falls down. She rushes ove.r*)

JENNY: Are you okay?!

BOB: Yes, student. I'm okay.

(FISK *and* HAYS *enter, see* BOB *on the ground.*)

FISK: What the hell...?

HAYS: Relax. Let me show you how it's done. (*To* BOB) Taking a break, are we?

BOB: We are? Thank you, boss. (*He relaxes.*)

FISK: (*To* HAYS) So that's how it's done, huh? (*To* BOB) Get up, Bob.

BOB: But, boss, bigger boss say I take break.

FISK: I'm countermanding that order, Bob. Get up.

BOB: Yes, boss. (*He stands.*)

FISK: Break's not for another hour. Get back to work.

BOB: Yes, boss.

(*As* BOB *gets back to work,* DIEGO *and* EDDIE *enter, not yet aware of what's playing out with the workers.* EDDIE *has his small backpack with him.*)

DIEGO: How many more lessons are there?

EDDIE: Tired?

DIEGO: A little.

EDDIE: That's good. One must know one's limitations. Only then can you work to overcome them.

DIEGO: I gotta say, though, I wish we were just done already. I need to kick me some butt.

EDDIE: Limitation numbers twenty-four and twenty-five: impatience and bad grammar.

(FISK *notices* EDDIE *and* DIEGO.)

FISK: What the hell are those two doing together?

HAYS: Bear in mind I'm counting on him to cough up some much needed funds.

FISK: You are one greedy woman.

HAYS: And I guess you just do it all for fun?

FISK: You got that right. Watch this. (*He approaches* DIEGO *and* EDDIE.) Hey. Janitor.

EDDIE: Yes, sir?

(FISK *turns over a trash can or some other mess-inducing action*)

FISK: Looks like you've got a mess to clean up.

(EDDIE *checks* FISK'*s pants.*)

EDDIE: You messed yourself, sir? Here, let me help.

FISK: Get away, you, you, you...Mexican! There! That mess!

EDDIE: Oh. Okay.

(EDDIE *starts cleaning the mess, much to* DIEGO'*s chagrin.* BOB *helps* EDDIE.)

FISK: How you doing, Mister Cervantes?

DIEGO: (*Seething*) Fine.

HAYS: Diego, so good to see you.

DIEGO: Headmaster.

HAYS: Do stop by sometime...and bring your checkbook!

(HAYS *laughs; she and* FISK *exit. Both* DIEGO *and* JENNY *are disgusted by the whole display.*)

JENNY: Mister Cervantes, you have to do something.

DIEGO: I know, Jenny...I know.

JENNY: So do it!

(JENNY *exits.* BOB *and* EDDIE *are still cleaning up the mess.*)

EDDIE: Thank you, Bob.

BOB: My pleasure...Mister Zorro.

DIEGO: What the—?

EDDIE: You know of Zorro?

BOB: I have watched you. (*He mimes a bit of swordplay. To* DIEGO) And you. (*To both*) I think at first you just crazy. But other men, the ones from this great Western land of yours, they tell me of Zorro. That he is gone for long time. Due to return soon. (*To* DIEGO) And then I see you practicing Zs everywhere.

DIEGO: I haven't been doing that...much

EDDIE: (*To* BOB) Well. Looks like you have a bit of Zorro in you—The Fox. You are quite clever.

BOB: Me? No! Really?

EDDIE: (*To* DIEGO) To simply rail against injustice is not enough. You must be clever enough to know when to take action. There is a time and a place for everything.

(BOB *grabs a sharp stick and begins wielding it like a sword.*)

BOB: Fight me, Zorro!

EDDIE: Sorry, no.

BOB: Yes! Playfight me so I can tell friends!

(BOB *gets another stick, throws it at* EDDIE'*s feet*)

BOB: Come on!

EDDIE: No, Bob.

BOB: Pick it up!

EDDIE: I couldn't.

BOB: (*As* EL MONSTRUO *said in opening scene*) Podrias. De veras, podrias.

(*Light change. Something in* EDDIE *shifts as he only sees* BOB *take on* EL MONSTRUO'*s attitude.* EDDIE *picks up the stick.*)

DIEGO: What are you doing?

EDDIE: Don't you see him? He's here.

DIEGO: It's just Bob.

EDDIE: No, it's not.

BOB: That's it. Fight!

DIEGO: You're not really going to—

EDDIE: It's the only way with you, Monstruo.

(*It's clear that* EDDIE *is about to do serious damage to* BOB *who is still unaware of what's going on.*)

EDDIE: This will only hurt for a second.

(DIEGO *leaps into action and swiftly disarms* EDDIE. BOB *is frightened,* EDDIE *is disoriented.*)

DIEGO: Good one, Bob. We got him. That was good, wasn't it, Eddie?

EDDIE: Yeah. It was good.

DIEGO: Bob, do you mind...?

BOB: Yes, yes...I go now. (*He exits.*)

DIEGO: You were going to gut him, weren't you?

(*EDDIE's face reveals nothing. Finally...*)

EDDIE: My backpack. Bring it over here.

DIEGO: You're not going to do something stupid, are you?

EDDIE: My backpack. *Por favor.*

(DIEGO *brings* EDDIE *his backpack.*)

EDDIE: I broke the oath. It is clearly past my time. And you saved a man's life. I have something for you. (*He pulls out a bundle of black clothing.*) This is yours now.

(DIEGO *opens the bundle, holds up the black mask of* ZORRO.)

(*Lights down*)

END OF ACT ONE

ACT TWO

Scene One

(School grounds. A few days later. JENNY *is walking in one direction,* HAYS *in the other.* JENNY *sees her coming and summons her courage.)*

JENNY: Headmaster?

HAYS: Yes. *(Searching her memory)* Ms...Summers?

JENNY: Winters.

HAYS: Whatever. What can I do for you? But make it quick, I have a pole-dance—I mean, a Pilates class to get to.

JENNY: Yes, ma'am. Um...it's just...a few of us have, uh...noticed that the workers don't be seem to be getting breaks during the day.

HAYS: That's their choice, Ms Winters. The more they work, the more they make. I can't stop them from earning the money they need, now can I?

JENNY: No, but...aren't there rules about this? Laws that say employers must—

HAYS: Ms Winters, stop right there! You are just a teenager—

JENNY: That doesn't mean—

HAYS: Do not interrupt me! This is my school and I am the decider, not you! Do you understand!?

JENNY: Yes—

HAYS: And while we're on the subject—your family hasn't exactly been generous when it comes to contributions for the Reconstruction Project! If you know what's good for you, you'll go home today and have a little talk with your parents about your future here!

(JENNY *is now almost invisible to the naked eye.*)

HAYS: And I most certainly don't want to ever hear you mention the workers again, is that clear?

(*Suddenly,* DIEGO *as* ZORRO *enters in an incredible fashion—he is dressed in his full regalia. But instead of a sword he carries a whip.*)

ZORRO: Headmaster Hays. Allow me to introduce myself...

JENNY: Zorro!

(HAYS *breaks out into laughter.*)

HAYS: Where's the camera? Come on, where is it? (*To* ZORRO) That was terrific! You had me going for a second there! I can't wait to see the expression on my face! So what is this, that show the kids watch... Punk You! —isn't that it!? (*To* JENNY) Oh, and I bet you were in on it! (*To* ZORRO) Oh, dear, is it possible to edit out the earlier conversation—before you came in so magnificently?

ZORRO: There are no cameras. This is not a television show. I am Zorro.

HAYS: Zorro? *The* Zorro?

ZORRO: *This* Zorro.

HAYS: Semantics. So, you're Zorro.

JENNY: How many times do you want him to say it?

HAYS: (*To* JENNY) Shut up!

ZORRO: I can't allow you to talk to her like that.

HAYS: This is insane—I'm calling security.

(HAYS *reaches for her cell phone.* ZORRO *pulls out his whip.*)

ZORRO: No, you're not!

(ZORRO *attempts to use the whip to snap the phone out of* HAYS's *hand, but instead it hits something else not even remotely near her.*)

HAYS: You want me to show you how to use that thing?

ZORRO: Hold on...

(ZORRO *tries again, this time hitting something else, making even more of a mess*)

HAYS: This is absurd! Wait! I know who you are!

JENNY: He's Zorro!

HAYS: He thinks he is! Ten years ago there was a man who thought he was Zorro. Wreaked havoc all over the state. They finally caught him and institutionalized him. (*To* ZORRO) It's you, isn't it?

(ZORRO *hesitates. With new resolve he tries again, succeeding in snapping the cell phone out of her hand*)

HAYS: Oww! Run away!

(HAYS *runs away.* ZORRO *uses her exit as a diversion to also exit in another direction.*)

JENNY: That was the coolest thing I've ever seen—

(JENNY *turns—*ZORRO *has disappeared.*)

JENNY: Where'd he go? (*She exits.*)

(*A moment passes;* EDDIE *wheels on Tornado. Dejected, miserable, he turns back to take one last look at the Academy. He sighs and exits*)

Scene Two

(HAYS's *office.* FISK *is slicing off the "heads" of effigies of public personalities—Hilary Clinton, Barack Obama, John McCain, Oprah, or whoever is most current, with his samurai sword.*)

FISK: Take that! ...And that! ...Let's not forget—hghhhh! And this is for aaaaarrrrhhhh!

(HAYS *runs in, she's out of breath and hysterical.*)

HAYS: John, help me! There's a madman out there! He whipped me, John, he whipped me!

FISK: But you like that.

HAYS: Not by some stranger! (*Beat*) A complete stranger. You have to get him, you have to kill him! Kill him, John, kill him!!!

FISK: Whoa, whoa, whoa—slow down there, hon—you gotta get a grip.

HAYS: You don't understand—it's Zorro!

FISK: Zorro?

HAYS: Well, no, not THE Zorro. THIS Zorro!

FISK: Come again?

HAYS: He's just crazy, okay?! You've got to hunt him down and skin him alive! Filet him! Slice him up into tiny pieces! Cook him on a spit!

(FISK *slaps* HAYS. *She comes back to her senses...somewhat.*)

FISK: Can you be rational?

HAYS: Yes. I think so.

FISK: Good.

HAYS: John, I'm afraid. What if he finds out about us—I mean, isn't that what Zorro does?

FISK: Francine, do you need another slap?

HAYS: I don't know. Maybe. Just a little one.

(FISK *doesn't slap her.*)

FISK: We're obviously dealing with a lunatic.

HAYS: I think it's the Zorro they put in the loony bin.

FISK: Oh. *That* Zorro. Either he escaped and is back at it...or it's a copy-cat situation. Or he's just a moron.

HAYS: Should we call the police?

FISK: Negatory.

HAYS: What about the nuthouse? Let's call them!

FISK: Again, negatory. Look, let me have some fun. I'll take care of him.

(HAYS *is getting turned on.*)

HAYS: Oh, yeah?

FISK: Oh, yeah.

(HAYS *gropes* FISK, *but he's harder to get excited than usual.*)

HAYS: Tell me again what we're going to do when we withdraw our money and move to Fiji....

FISK: Francine, not now.

HAYS: Tell me what you're going to do to me with that boiling hot coconut oil...

FISK: Do you hear me saying no?

HAYS: (*Not hearing him*) And that roll of razor sharp wire...dipped in chocolate...

FISK: I said no!

(FISK *puts an end to* HAYS's *advances a little too roughly.*)

HAYS: There's someone else, isn't there?

FISK: Yes. No! I just want to concentrate on getting this Zorro character. You don't want everything we've worked for to blow up in our faces, do you?

HAYS: No, of course not.

FISK: Then let me do what I've been trained to do.

HAYS: Be a security guard?

(FISK *grabs* HAYS *by the neck; she can't breathe.*)

FISK: I am more than a security guard!! I am an artist—the body is my canvas, the sword my brush....

(FISK *realizes he's stepped over the line. He releases* HAYS, *she coughs.*)

FISK: I'm sorry, darling. I just got...worked up...you know, about hunting this guy down. Please forgive me.

HAYS: (*Through her coughs*) It's...okay...I...love...you...

FISK: And I love you.

Scene Three

(DIEGO's *classroom. The next day. He is finishing a lecture;* JENNY *and other* STUDENTS *are there, hanging on his every word.*)

DIEGO: So...can you reverse-engineer software? Some believe you should be able to make copies of someone else's work. But what if that's illegal? (*Beat*) And if something is illegal, isn't it our responsibility to bring about legality and make things right? By any means? And that, my peeps, wraps it up for the day.

(JENNY *stands and applauds, the other* STUDENTS *joining her—they improvise a chant/rap*)

JENNY & STUDENTS: Cervantes, Cervantes, go, go, go! Cervantes, Cervantes, go, go, go!

DIEGO: Thank you. Thank you.

STUDENT #1: Hey, Mister Cervantes, what do you think about Zorro?!

STUDENT #2: Come on, that is so bogus—I think Jenny made the whole thing up.

JENNY: I did not!

STUDENT #3: Did he sound like Antonio Banderas?

JENNY: No. Hotter.

(*The class laughs.*)

DIEGO: They say he escaped from a mental institution—what do you think of that?

(DIEGO's *comment subdues the class, the mood becomes somber.*)

JENNY: You know what? I don't care if he escaped from Mars. I know what I saw. I know what I felt. As far as I'm concerned he's Zorro. (*Beat*) All we need to do now is get him to help the workers.

STUDENT #2: Whatever.

(*The bell rings. The* STUDENTS *leave,* JENNY *bringing up the rear.*)

DIEGO: Jenny. Thank you.

JENNY: For what?

DIEGO: Nothing. See you later.

JENNY: Bye.

(*As* JENNY *exits,* OLIVIA *enters.*)

JENNY: Isn't it exciting, Ms Baker? About Zorro.

OLIVIA: It certainly is.

DIEGO: You don't sound too excited.

OLIVIA: Oh, I don't know, I just find it all very convenient. Ever since this Zorro person appeared, no one's seemed to notice how the day-laborers are being treated. It feels wrong. Like someone's doing this to distract us.

DIEGO: Wow. I hadn't thought of it like that.

OLIVIA: No one has.

DIEGO: Except you.

OLIVIA: He needs to be unmasked. Someone's got to prove that it's Hays and Fisk who are behind it.

DIEGO: What would happen if he was unmasked and... he turns out to be some regular guy who's just trying to make a difference?

OLIVIA: I'd tell him that there are better ways to go about it. All he's doing now is making a spectacle of himself.

(DIEGO's *head is spinning*.)

OLIVIA: Are you okay?

DIEGO: I'm fine. (*Beat*) You still need proof, right?

OLIVIA: Well, yes, that would certainly help. But in lieu of getting that proof, and since my petition died on the vine, I've realized I need to step this up. We're going to have a rally. Show the world what's really happening here.

DIEGO: When is it?

OLIVIA: I don't know yet, I'm still planning it. All I know is that it can't be some little thing here that Hays can easily silence. I've got to think big, you know what I mean?

DIEGO: Yeah, I do.

OLIVIA: Are you with me?

DIEGO: I am.

(OLIVIA *impulsively kisses* DIEGO *on the lips. He practically swoons*.)

OLIVIA: Hmm. Not bad.

(OLIVIA *exits.* DIEGO *sighs heavily*.)

Scene Four

(School grounds. EDDIE, dressed in vestiges of the homeless, is alone with Tornado the shopping cart, now packed with his things. BOB enters.)

BOB: Please excuse, can we talk...Mister Zorro?

EDDIE: My name is Eddie. Eddie Reyes. Not Zorro.

BOB: I understand. My name not really is Bob. But I say it is because is convenient.

EDDIE: Convenient. What do you mean?

BOB: *(Hushed)* In my country...I am Russian soldier. They order I should kill Chechnyans. I no kill peoples who only want a home. I no kill children. So I run. To mile high country.

EDDIE: That's a good story, Bob. So, tell me, why not just let people know? I'm sure there are Russians in the country who would welcome you.

BOB: And bring back nightmares? That's why I'm Bob.

EDDIE: You're a smart man.

BOB: And you. I call you Eddie because for you is convenient, too. *(Beat)* Everybody talking about you.

EDDIE: It wasn't me.

BOB: *(with a wink)* Sure, sure.

EDDIE: Bob, haven't you heard? Zorro is just a man who escaped from an asylum.

BOB: Sure, sure. *(Re: Tornado)* Tornado?

EDDIE: What? No. Shopping cart.

BOB: Sure, sure.

EDDIE: Bob, I'd like to be left alone, if that's alright with you.

BOB: (*Beat*) Workers they have no faces. No families. No past. No future. That's what people think. This you can change. You think about this, yes?

(BOB *exits.* DIEGO *enters, sees* EDDIE's *belongings in Tornado.*)

DIEGO: Is this how it's going to be? You give me this... amazing gift...then you disappear?

EDDIE: A lunatic who calls himself Zorro has escaped from the asylum.

DIEGO: Yeah, I've heard. You're a genius.

EDDIE: I'm the butt of a joke.

DIEGO: Don't you see, it's working. We've got people not knowing what to think, that's just where we want them—off-guard.

EDDIE: They want me committed.

DIEGO: Does Bob want you committed?

EDDIE: No.

DIEGO: My best student doesn't want you committed. And I bet a lot more will come around once they've seen Zorro in action.

EDDIE: You don't understand. The nightmares. They are frequent. And frighteningly real. I'm going back to the place where bad dreams just...pharmaceutically dissolve. (*Beat*) You know how they're saying I was put away? I put myself away.

(*Silence*)

DIEGO: It doesn't matter. What matters is the hope on the faces of the people of La Reina de Los Angeles when they see that Z carved into the wanted sign of Zorro. What matters is Basil Rathbone as Captain Pasquale getting what he deserves. What matters is seeing oppression met with justice. And what matters...

is what I see in the faces of Bob and Jenny and a whole lot of other people around here. (*To shopping cart*) Hey wassup, Tornado?

EDDIE: Did I say you could talk to him? (*Getting his things together*) Before I met you I'd decided I was going to just be a regular person again. Living in that half-awake, half-asleep state. Instead, you fully woke me up. Thank you for the brief moment of lucidity. But now...it's time to go back to sleep.

DIEGO: You can't do that.

EDDIE: Watch me.

DIEGO: (*Calling after him*) Zorro doesn't give up!

EDDIE: This one does.

DIEGO: He's alive as long as someone's behind the mask!

EDDIE: Zorro is dead. Long live Zorro.

(EDDIE *is gone.* DIEGO *is alone.*)

Scene Five

(*School grounds. Another day.* BOB *and the* WORKERS *are in the midst of a job that involves various tools: shovels, hoes, spades, etc. that are used in a percussive manner, becoming a production number.* HAYS *enters and watches, enjoying their bodies.*)

BOB: Big boss!

HAYS: Me?

BOB: Yes, you, big boss! Come join!

HAYS: I couldn't.

BOB: Yes, come, big boss! Join us!

HAYS: Well. Maybe just...

(HAYS *throws herself into it; the* WORKERS *cheer her on.* OLIVIA *enters, can't believe what she's seeing.* HAYS *notices her and stops immediately.*)

HAYS: (*To* BOB *and* WORKERS) Stop it.

(BOB *and* WORKERS *continue.*)

HAYS: Stop it!

(BOB *and* WORKERS *continue.*)

HAYS: STOP IT!!!!!

(*Everyone except for* BOB *stops.* HAYS *grabs a shovel and hits him with it.* JENNY, *who entered sometime during all this, runs up to him.*)

JENNY: Are you okay?

BOB: Yes, angel of mine, I'm okay.

HAYS: You heard me! I specifically asked everyone to stop, and, and...he wouldn't listen! (*To* OLIVIA) What do you want?

OLIVIA: I just wish I'd taken a picture.

HAYS: But you didn't, did you? (*To* BOB, *solicitous*) Are you alright, dear fellow?

BOB: Yes, big boss.

HAYS: See? He's alright. It was just a little... miscommunication. (*To* BOB) You realize it was just an accident, don't you?

BOB: Yes, big boss.

OLIVIA: (*To* BOB) How can I help you if you won't help yourself?

BOB: Time and a place, dear lady teacher.

OLIVIA: Right. (*To* HAYS) You want to know what I want?

(HAYS *walks* OLIVIA *away from everyone.*)

HAYS: Not especially, but I did ask, so...go ahead.

OLIVIA: I want you to quit. But first I want you to apologize to the people you've been taking advantage of. I want you to pay them what they deserve. And then I want you to quit.

HAYS: Isn't that interesting? I want you to quit.

OLIVIA: I'm not going to quit.

HAYS: I could fire you. But that wouldn't look very good on your record, now would it?

OLIVIA: On what grounds?

HAYS: You've broken countless by-laws with your little crusade. Plus I know if I look hard enough, I'll find some bones in your closet.

OLIVIA: You are the biggest b—

HAYS: (*Interrupting*) Hey! Little pitchers have big ears. So. Friday is the field trip to those ridiculous Indian Burial Grounds. Seeing as how you're the history teacher and no one else gives a damn, your presence is needed. Why don't we consider that your last day, hm?

(OLIVIA *says nothing*)

HAYS: Excellent.

(DIEGO *as* ZORRO *enters in another spectacular way.*)

JENNY: Zorro!

BOB: Zorro!

WORKERS: Zorro!

OLIVIA: Zorro.

HAYS: Zorro?!

WORKER #1: Kick her butt, Zorro!

WORKERS: Ya, kick her butt!

ZORRO: Patience, my friends!

(HAYS *holds up a little gizmo.*)

HAYS: I've activated this C I A-approved G P S tracking signal. Fisk will be here in less than a minute.

ZORRO: (*To* JENNY) Why do they always tell you things like that?

JENNY: Cinematic convention. You just gotta go with it.

ZORRO: Right. (*To* HAYS) I thought I warned you about this sort of behavior.

HAYS: What are you, my father?!

ZORRO: Clearly you have father issues, yes?

HAYS: I am so going to have you locked up.

WORKERS: Kick her butt!!!

HAYS: You wouldn't dare. Not in front of all these witnesses.

ZORRO: All the more reason to...

(ZORRO *does the trademark branding of the Z on* HAYS'*s clothes.*)

HAYS: Aaaaaaaaaaa!!!

ZORRO: Next time the consequences will be far worse. (*To* OLIVIA) Ms Baker.

OLIVIA: You know my name?

ZORRO: You are well known. Thank you for your efforts.

OLIVIA: (*Despite herself*) Thank you for yours.

(HAYS *is so busy trying to cover herself she's hardly aware of* ZORRO *exiting. A moment later,* FISK *enters with his sword ready for action.*)

FISK: Where is he?! Where'd he go?!

(*Everybody points in different directions.*)

FISK: Damnit! Get out of my sight!

(*He brandishes the sword.*)

I said, get the hell out of here!!

HAYS: Look what he did to my suit! Need I remind you this is a Mosimo!

FISK: Need I remind you I don't give a damn.

(HAYS *gasps.*)

HAYS: Don't you dare speak to me like that!

FISK: Don't you dare!

BOB: Boss, maybe you think two more times before speaking. Big boss very strong. (*Showing his own "wound"*) Look.

(*That's it.* FISK *is done with it all.*)

FISK: Okay. By the time I get to "one" you will all be gone. Ten, nine, eight...

OLIVIA: Come on, Jenny, let's go.

JENNY: He's bluffing.

FISK: Seven...six...five...

OLIVIA: Doesn't matter—let's go.

(OLIVIA *practically drags* JENNY *offstage as everybody also obeys* FISK.)

FISK: Four, three, two...one.

(BOB *is the only who hasn't left*)

FISK: Bob.

BOB: Boss.

FISK: Why haven't you left?

BOB: I know you, boss. People like you.

FISK: Oh, really.

BOB: Sad, angry. You are, yes?

FISK: I've had enough of you, Bob.

BOB: Yes, boss. I know.

(FISK *talks into his walkie-talkie.*)

FISK: There's a maniac in a black cape—he's got my sword! I think he's going to hurt one of the workers! Get over to the south gate A-SAP!!

BOB: You make mistake.

FISK: I disagree.

BOB: Is okay, boss. I understand.

FISK: Doubt it.

(FISK *runs his sword through* BOB, *who slumps to the ground. Sound of siren closing in.*)

FISK: Excuse me, Bob.

(FISK *exits.* EDDIE *enters from opposite direction with Tornado; he doesn't yet see* BOB)

EDDIE: (*To Tornado*) Why do I listen to you, Tornado? Yes, I know, I was a bit rash, and maybe I shouldn't have said all that to Diego, but...Bob?

(EDDIE *rushes to* BOB)

BOB: (*At death's door*) Boss Fisk.

FISK: (*Offstage*)

He's over this way!

(EDDIE *puts* BOB *into Tornado; they all exit.*)

Scene Six

(HAYS' *office. She, in a panic, is stuffing money into a bag.*)

HAYS: Must leave fast, must leave fast, must...make reservations at the Fiji Four Seasons.

(FISK *enters*)

FISK: What are you doing?

HAYS: What's it look like I'm doing?

FISK: Panicking.

HAYS: No, I'm simply liquidating and leaving.

FISK: Do you have any idea how stupid that is?

HAYS: Do you have any idea how dangerous that Zorro fellow is?

FISK: That's true, he did kill Bob just now.

HAYS: What?!

FISK: Stabbed him with my own sword.

HAYS: Isn't that your sword in your hand?

FISK: He dropped it at the scene of the crime.

HAYS: How convenient. And brilliant.

FISK: Affirmative. There's one thing, though.

HAYS: What's that, my darling?

FISK: Bob's body. It's gone. Vanished.

HAYS: Zorro must've taken it.

FISK: My thought exactly. And that's why I called the guys over at The Bell Jar Psychiatric Hospital. They should be here soon.

HAYS: But how do you know Zorro is still on the grounds?

FISK: Bob bit the dust on his watch. He'll turn up.

(EDDIE *as* ZORRO *crashes in; he's improvised a costume made out of whatever he could find. Instead of a sword he has a car antenna that he's wrapped a rag and duct tape around for a handle.*)

ZORRO: Headmaster.

FISK: That's him, that's Zorro?

HAYS: He doesn't look the same.

ZORRO: My usual garb is at the cleaners—don't let these fool you—I am still Zorro.

HAYS: Your voice is different, too.

ZORRO: I have many voices.

FISK: Okay, grandma, I hope you have many swords because that one is pitiful.

ZORRO: A sword is only as pitiful as the man who wields it.

FISK: This is going to be way too easy.

(ZORRO *notices the money in front of* HAYS.)

ZORRO: That's a lot of money. I don't suppose it's yours.

HAYS: Kill him, John, kill him.

FISK: In due time, my pussycat.

ZORRO: I am here to redress the crimes of oppression perpetrated upon the day laborers, the students, and the faculty of the Academy of the Desert. And especially for Bob. Your violence against him was an act of cowardice. Your reign of terror is about to end, Mister Fisk.

FISK: I guess due time has arrived. I am about to gut you.

ZORRO: I thought I would never hear myself utter these words again but...well may you try.

FISK: So, before I do that...who the hell are you?

ZORRO: I am something you'll never understand.

HAYS: What are you waiting for—gut him!

ZORRO: En garde.

FISK: *En garde* it is.

(*The swordfight begins.* FISK *cheats and* ZORRO'*s sword is made irrelevant; he defends himself with anything he can find. But* ZORRO's *resourcefulness is not enough to vanquish* FISK, *and at the moment when it looks like* FISK *is about to win...)*

FISK: *Adios,* Zorro...

(The men in WHITE COATS *burst in.* HAYS *hides the money.)*

FISK: Aww, crap!

WHITE COAT #1: Hey there, Eddie, long time no see.

HAYS: Eddie?

ZORRO: No, not now! Let me go out the way I was meant to!

WHITE COAT #2: Sorry, but it looks like you got carried away this time.

ZORRO: Please?!

WHITE COAT #1: Let it go.

(They subdue EDDIE *with little effort.)*

FISK: Wait.

(He unmasks ZORRO.*)*

Eddie the janitor.

EDDIE: Who did you expect, Tyrone Power?

FISK: This man killed a day laborer by the name of Bob. Except there's no body. But we're working on that.

WHITE COAT #2: No kidding.

EDDIE: He's lying.

HAYS: Face it, Mister Janitor, you're going to prison or to the loony bin.

FISK: And either way's fine by me.

WHITE COAT #1: Come on now.

EDDIE: Please don't do this.

WHITE COAT #2: Sorry, Eddie...it's our job.

(DIEGO *rushes in.*)

DIEGO: I saw the ambulance, what's going—

(*He goes numb on seeing what's happening.*)

Eddie?

FISK: Your buddy here killed Bob. Probably chopped him up into tiny pieces. Oh, yeah, and he thinks he's Zorro.

EDDIE: I AM ZORRO.

HAYS: The poor man.

WHITE COAT #1: Don't worry, we'll straighten this all out soon enough. (*To* EDDIE) It's time.

(EDDIE *lets himself be escorted out.*)

HAYS: (*To* DIEGO) Don't you have students to bore?

FISK: Yeah. Get along there, little doggie.

(DIEGO *considers drastic measures, but thinks twice.*)

DIEGO: Excuse me.

(*He exits.*)

Scene Seven

(*The Desert, two days later, under an overcast sky.*
STUDENTS *enter with* JENNY, OLIVIA, DIEGO, HAYS *and* FISK. *Both* DIEGO *and* FISK *carry long bags strapped over their shoulders.*)

OLIVIA: (*To the students*) Ancient fire rings have been discovered here, carbon dated to be three-thousand-three-hundred years old.

STUDENT: That's pretty old for a barbeque.

OLIVIA: Quite so. The Ute Indians were likely the tribe that regularly buried their dead just over that hill.

(A STUDENT *picks up a stick.)*

OLIVIA: The Utes have a religious aversion to handling thunder wood-that's wood from a tree struck by lightning-and believe that the thunder beings would strike down any Ute Indian that touched or handled such wood.

(A crack of thunder. The STUDENT *drops the stick.)*

STUDENTS: Whoa.

FISK: *(To* DIEGO*)* What's in the bag?

DIEGO: Camping equipment. What's in yours?

FISK: Peacemaker. I never leave home without her.

JENNY: *(To* OLIVIA*)* It's breathtaking here!

(Several STUDENTS *make lewd kissing sounds.)*

JENNY: *(To* STUDENTS*)* I am not! And if you keep doing that...I'm going to reach down your throats and rip out your lungs.

(The STUDENTS *stop immediately.)*

OLIVIA: Jenny. I've never heard you talk like that.

JENNY: Sorry, Ms Baker. I'm just so mad about what happened.

OLIVIA: About Bob?

JENNY: I can't believe Zorro would do that!

OLIVIA: Me, neither.

JENNY: What do you think, Mister Cervantes?

DIEGO: About what?

JENNY: Zorro!

DIEGO: Oh. I don't see why he'd hurt Bob. I know I wouldn't.

OLIVIA: That's because you wouldn't hurt a fly. I mean, come on, a man who runs around with a sword is eventually going to hurt someone. There are less violent ways to get things done. Peaceful ways.

DIEGO: What if those peaceful ways don't work?

OLIVIA: So you were seduced by Zorro, too, huh?

DIEGO: Seduced by him *too*?

OLIVIA: (*Flustered*) I kissed you, not him.

DIEGO: Right.

OLIVIA: Anyway, they've locked him up. We won't be seeing Zorro again.

(HAYS *and* FISK *have stepped aside from the group.*)

FISK: Aren't you glad I didn't let you cut and run?

HAYS: Yes, yes, you were right, I was wrong and I'll never doubt you again.

FISK: Wiser words were never spoken. (*Beat*) You did put those...dirty clothes...somewhere safe?

HAYS: Of course I did. They're right over there in my car.

FISK: What?!

HAYS: I have an appointment this afternoon. A new Chinese laundry service I just found.

FISK: Oh. Okay. Make sure they get the stains out.

HAYS: Oh, I'll definitely do that.

(*The sky darkens, the wind picks up.*)

JENNY: Looks like a storm's about to hit.

OLIVIA: That's it.

DIEGO: What?

OLIVIA: Look around you. What do you see?

DIEGO: Shades of red. Orange. Ancient spirits whispering...

(The wind begins to howl.)

DIEGO: Howling. Ashamed of who we've become. Ashamed of the way we treat each other. Just like how we treat the land...like it was disposable.

OLIVIA: *(Impressed)* Well. Yes. Absolutely. And that's exactly why this is the perfect place to make a statement.

DIEGO: Statement?

OLIVIA: Remember? The rally I told you about? It's happening. Right here. Right now.

DIEGO: I don't know, Olivia.

OLIVIA: What's not to know? This is how it works. The greatest movements in history are started by regular people who've had enough. And we have had enough. We make our stand right here in Nature's bosom. We'll raise such a stink even the spirits will come out to cheer us on.

DIEGO: I still don't know. Fisk is only looking for an excuse.

OLIVIA: Then I'll give it to him and we'll see how brave he really is. *(To all, including the audience)* Excuse me. Excuse me! I have something to say!

(The STUDENTS *start to gather.* DIEGO *slips away.)*

OLIVIA: My name is Olivia Baker and I'm a teacher at Academy of the Desert!

*(*OLIVIA *notices that* DIEGO *has disappeared.)*

OLIVIA: Diego?

HAYS: What is she doing?

FISK: It's not good, I'll tell you that.

OLIVIA: There is a plaque on the Statue of Liberty. On it is written a poem by Emma Lazarus. And I quote. "Give me your tired, your poor, your..."

HAYS: Ms Baker, I must ask you to stop what you're doing.

OLIVIA: This is Headmaster Hays. The sadist next to her is John Fisk. Together they have conspired to bilk private donors by preying upon—

HAYS: That's it, you're fired!

OLIVIA: Undocumented workers who have come to our country in search of—

FISK: Did you not hear the lady?! You are to cease and desist from this blatantly illegal demonstration!

OLIVIA: What's illegal is the graft and corruption of these two individuals you see standing before you!

HAYS: John, shut her up!

OLIVIA: That's right, shut me up! Just like you do to anyone who dares raise their voice against you!

JENNY: She's right! I've seen what they're doing! The workers are too frightened to speak up because their livelihoods depend on crappy jobs like the ones Academy of the Desert is offering them!

HAYS: (*Re:* OLIVIA) She is a disgruntled employee who has been fired. (*Re:* JENNY)And she is a disgruntled student who has just been expelled! Who are you going to believe?! Me or them?!

(*One of the* STUDENTS *throws a juice box at* HAYS.)

HAYS: Oww! Who did that?!

FISK: You heard the lady! Who did it?!

ZORRO: I did!

(*Everyone looks up high to the rocks where the voice came from—it's...*)

ALL: Zorro!

FISK: Another one?

(His best entrance yet, DIEGO as ZORRO lands with his sword poised for action. FISK pulls out his sword.)

ZORRO: The question is: what are you going to do?

FISK: Make you squeal like a stuck pig. And that's just for starters. *(To all)* You've all seen this man—this man in a costume—a copycat wannabe—challenge me to...

(Another STUDENT throws another juice box, this one at FISK.)

FISK: That's it!

(FISK starts to charge toward the students, ZORRO blocks his way.)

ZORRO: Why don't you pick on someone with a sword your own size?

FISK: My pleasure.

(FISK and ZORRO begin a swordfight. The STUDENTS cheer as HAYS begins to make a cell phone call, but is stopped by JENNY. Meanwhile OLIVIA quietly makes a call herself.)

FISK: You're pretty good...for a dead man!

(Thrusts and parries galore. ZORRO cuts the Z with his sword onto FISK.)

ZORRO: Looks like you need a new tailor.

(ZORRO is clearly winning now, so FISK begins fighting dirtier.)

ZORRO: Admit it, Fisk. You're outmatched!

FISK: Where'd you learn to fight like that?!

ZORRO: The Royal Court of Spain.

FISK: Is that part of the job description—crazy as a loon?

ZORRO: As a fox, perhaps.

(FISK *goes on the attack again.* ZORRO *repels him, making him look even more foolish.* FISK *grabs* OLIVIA, *holds the sword to her throat.*)

FISK: Drop your weapon! I said, drop it!

(ZORRO *puts down his sword.*)

FISK: Kick it over here.

(ZORRO *kicks his sword toward* FISK. FISK *releases* OLIVIA *and moves toward* ZORRO *to finish him off. At that very moment,* EDDIE *rushes on pushing Tornado with* BOB *in it—right into* FISK. ZORRO *retrieves his sword, the two men go at each other with everything they have and finally...* ZORRO *disarms* FISK *and has him at his mercy.*)

FISK: (*Sobbing*) Please don't kill me! Please!

(ZORRO *brings the blade even closer to* FISK.)

EDDIE: Zorro!

(ZORRO *looks at* EDDIE, *at* OLIVIA, *at everyone. He lowers his sword.*)

ZORRO: There are other ways. Peaceful ones.

(*Police sirens can be heard in the distance*)

ZORRO: Tie him up.

EDDIE: Don't mind if I do.

(HAYS *tries to make a run for it.* JENNY *displays some fancy footwork of her own and stops* HAYS.)

HAYS: (*Re:* FISK) He made me do it!

FISK: Francine!

HAYS: It was all his idea!

FISK: Check her car! There's at least fifty thousand in cash that's not hers!

HAYS: Judas!

FISK: Jezebel!

(EDDIE *stuffs rags into* FISK's *and* HAYS's *mouths*)

JENNY: Bob, we thought you were dead.

BOB: Mister...Eddie...very good first-aider.

JENNY: (*To* EDDIE) And didn't they lock you up?

EDDIE: I am a man of many skills.

ZORRO: (*To* EDDIE) How did you find us?

(EDDIE *takes the G P S tracker out of* HAYS' *pocket*)

EDDIE: (*To* HAYS) These work pretty well, you know.

(FISK *spits out his gag.*)

FISK: My father buried me up to my neck at the beach and left me for the seagulls! My mother stuffed a box of alka-seltzers into my mouth and made me drink club soda! My brother—

(HAYS *spits out her gag.*)

HAYS: He's lying! He doesn't have a brother!

JENNY: I know he is—I can smell it.

(JENNY *stuffs the rags further into their mouths.* OLIVIA *takes* ZORRO *aside.*)

OLIVIA: (*To* ZORRO) Thank you.

ZORRO: No. Thank you.

OLIVIA: I know who you are.

ZORRO: Yes, I know.

OLIVIA: You could've told me.

ZORRO: No, I couldn't.

OLIVIA: Yes, you could.

(OLIVIA *and* ZORRO *kiss.*)

JENNY: Zorro. The police are almost here.

ZORRO: (*To* JENNY) One of these days I'm going to show you a box.

JENNY: Okay.

(ZORRO *rejoins the group*)

EDDIE: And the student becomes the teacher again. The circle is complete.

(ZORRO *approaches* EDDIE.)

EDDIE: Do you remember when we met and I looked into your eyes? And how I wouldn't tell you what I saw in them?

ZORRO: Tell me now.

EDDIE: I saw a man in search of a compass. (*Beat*) I saw hope. A dream. A possibility. And a chance for redemption. Okay, the redemption was mainly for me, but it's good for you, too.

ZORRO: You saw a lot.

(EDDIE *and* ZORRO *embrace.*)

ZORRO: I'll miss you.

EDDIE: No, you won't, because Zorro will always be with you. (*Beat*) Bob. They say that in California there are great windmills that fill the horizon. Shall we go see them?

BOB: Yes. Let's go.

EDDIE: Come, Tornado.

(EDDIE *wheels* BOB *off and they exit. The sirens stop—the police have arrived.* ZORRO *looks up, taking in the desert.*)

ZORRO: (*To the spirits*) Please forgive our intrusion. (*To all*) May we find justice in us all! (*He makes a terrific exit.*)

END OF PLAY

www.ingramcontent.com/pod-product-compliance
Lightning Source LLC
Chambersburg PA
CBHW052212090426

42741CB00010B/2514